Flip Chart Magic!

—77 Energizing Ideas for Novices and Experts!—

A Seminar in a Book!

By Dave Arch and Ivar Torgrimson

With an introduction by:
Robert W. Pike, CSP

HRD Press • Amherst • Massachusetts

Published by:
HRD Press
22 Amherst Road
Amherst, MA 01002
1-800-822-2801 (U.S. and Canada)
1-413-253-3490 (FAX)
1-413-253-3488
http://www.hrdpress.com

ISBN 0-87425-507-4

Production services by Clark Riley

Cover design by Eileen Klockars

Editorial services by Suzanne Bay

Dedication

To our families for their patience during the work on this book.

To all left-brained, analytical presenters whose comments inspired this book to become a very sequential approach to learning how to design and draw effective flip charts.

TABLE OF CONTENTS

Flip Chart Magic!

WHERE TO FIND

INTRODUCTION

Welcome to this flip chart seminar-in-a-book! By combining your markers and this workbook, you will soon be dazzling your participants with increasingly effective flip charts!

If you only feel confident enough to draw stick figures, you will soon see that this book has been designed to sequentially move you through the steps of transforming your expertise with stick figures into a full repertoire of different graphics, borders, and lettering.

For a quick look at this process, use the lower right-hand corner of this page (and all the pages to follow) as a Flip Book! Let your thumb riffle the lower right hand corner of the pages from the front of the book to the back, and you'll get a very visual appreciation of the process that you'll soon be experiencing.

If you already feel fairly confident in your flip chart skills and merely want to add to those skills, the back half of this book is a more advanced approach to flip chart design and you'll find some NEW graphics, borders, and lettering to add to your own tool kit.

Between the basic and the advanced sections, you'll discover a very unique part of the book entitled "Flip Chart Fun." Here you will find two forgotten entertainment mediums of the 1940s and 50s brought up to date for your participants. Simple Chalk Talks and Doodles have been selected on a wide variety of different content applications.

If you glance for a moment at the Table of Contents, you will also notice that the six sections of the book have been divided into three divisions. The first, "Need to Know," is where you will find those pieces of information that are foundational to effective use of flip charts. The "Nice to Know" information includes those aspects of flip chart usage that build on those "must know" things — carrying the usefulness of the flip chart one step further. Finally, there is a list of resources in the "Where to Find" section that will help you make the most effective use of this and other training tools in your own presentations.

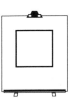

Flip Chart Magic!

And by the way, don't miss the bonus section, where you'll find seventeen transparency masters with a diversity of content-related graphics. By using these masters and an overhead projector, you'll soon be sheepishly receiving the praise of your participants for your artistic flip charts. Sure won't hurt your evaluations, either!

(There's no need to tell them how easy it is.)

May you find yourself having more fun than you ever imagined as you and your participants discover the wonders of ***Flip Chart Magic!***

Bob Pike

HOW TO USE THIS BOOK

This book is not for the naturally artistic. You will find it far too basic. Rather, it is for the left-brained analytical presenter. Beginning with the drawing of a stick figure, you will find yourself taken step-by-little-step through a very sequential growth process designed to build confidence with each new hands-on exercise and turn of the page.

If you feel shaky in your drawing skills, then please begin with page 3 and move your way page-by-page through the book. However, if you already have a fair amount of proficiency, please proceed to page 59 and discover NEW techniques to add to your toolkit, which can be found in the last half of the book.

Looking for some great come-back-from-break flip chart puzzlers? Check out the Doodles section, beginning on page 91.

Seeking some new ways to emphasize content in a very visual and dramatic fashion? Examine some of the Chalk Talks beginning on page 73.

Finally, please don't forget to use the section entitled Your Own Ideas! We've provided half a dozen pages so you can record your best graphics, borders, doodles, or chalk talks. They'll all be in one place for easy reference.

After you have worked your way through this book and accumulated your best ideas in this final section, you might find Your Own Ideas the most valuable of all!

Section One:

Flip Chart Design

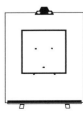

THE GRAPHIC

Let's get started! Please open the box of markers that came with your book, select your favorite-smelling marker, and on the next page, draw your very best stick figure. You can do it!

THE GRAPHIC

Congratulations! You did it! You have a proven ability to draw a 0, and a stick figure! That's all you need to be able to draw in order to begin. You have what it takes! Just rearrange the parts and you'll have the picture on the next page!"

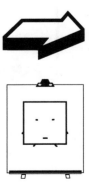

THE GRAPHIC

Now *you* try it! On the next few pages are the beginnings of some new flip chart graphics. Using the previous page as a pattern, move through the following pages, adding eyes, nose, mouth, arms, and legs to bring these figures to life. Enjoy yourself — it's really quite fun!

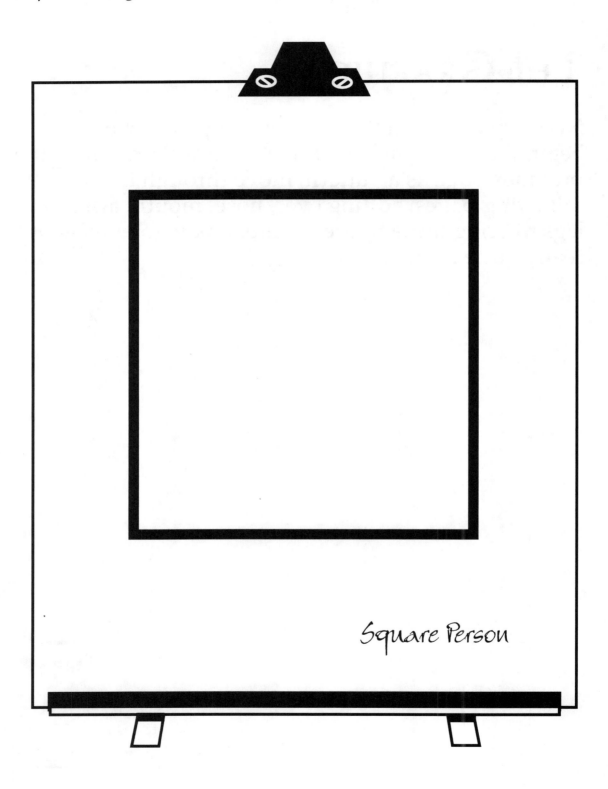

Square Person

Circle Person

Rectangle Person

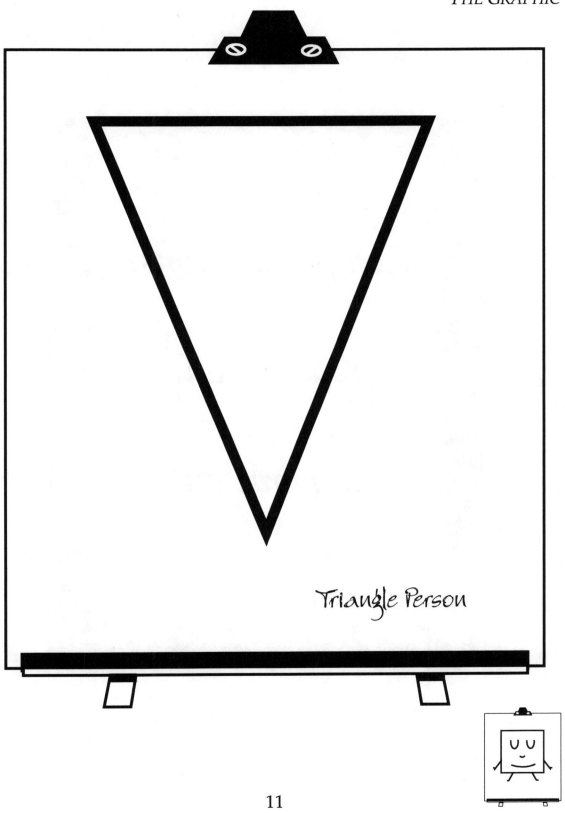

Triangle Person

Congratulations!

You're ready

to move on!

LET'S FACE IT!

In this age of active computer graphics, we must try to infuse our stationary flip chart graphics with as much action as we can. One of the best ways is through the communication of emotion in each and every graphic! Look at the next page and note the wide range of emotions we can communicate with the very same figures we've just drawn. Then move on to the following pages and use your marker to practice adding emotions to a new set of flip chart graphics. You *can* do it!

FACE IT!

Worried

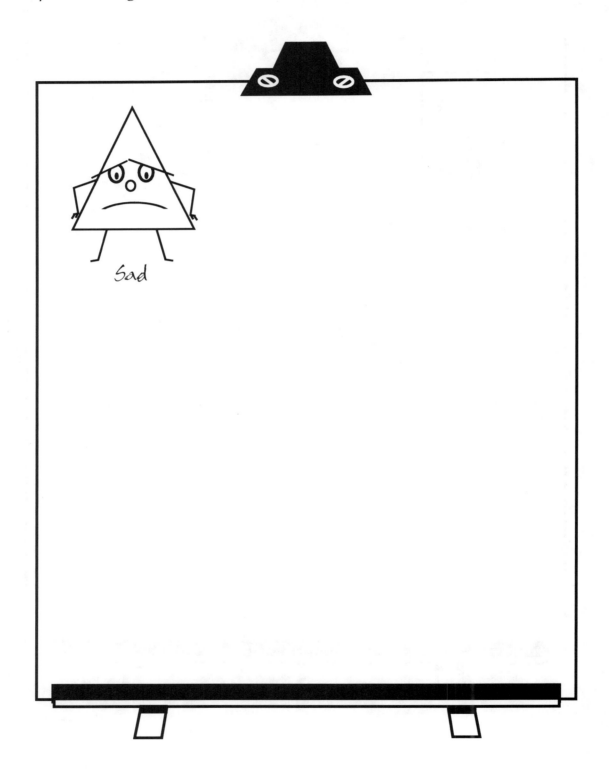

Sad

Ecstatic

Flip Chart Magic!

Embarrassed

Overwhelmed

Frustrated

Scared

21

Proud

Angry

THE COLOR

Color communicates! Look at the seven small flip charts below. Before turning the page, try opening your box of markers and selecting a single color that best communicates the message(s) printed below each flip chart. Then color the small flip chart with the color you selected. After coloring each flip chart, turn the page and compare your opinions with those of researchers.

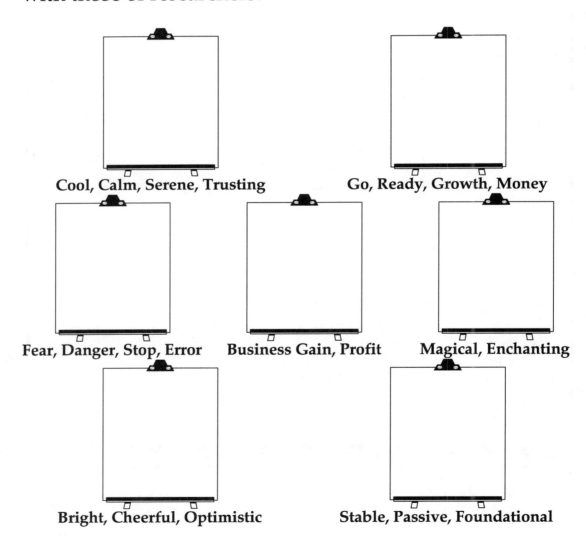

Cool, Calm, Serene, Trusting   Go, Ready, Growth, Money

Fear, Danger, Stop, Error   Business Gain, Profit   Magical, Enchanting

Bright, Cheerful, Optimistic   Stable, Passive, Foundational

RED is emotional. It can convey happiness, sadness, excitement, anxiety, desire, and passion, transcending cultural boundaries. Red heightens effectiveness, raises the pulse rate, and calls the audience to action!

BLUE (particularly the darker blue) has a calming effect and indicates a conservative approach to the information while maintaining credibility. The words *cool, calm, serene,* and *trusting* all capsulize our emotional feelings about the color blue. Blue is a more "vulnerable" color than black, and consequently will elicit more input from the participants. Blue takes the "hype" out of information, making it appear more credible to participants.

BLACK is a wonderful color for financial presentations signifying profit or gain in business. It also carries with it the emotion of what has already happened or what is in the past that cannot be changed. Black communicates an unshakable stability, and is certainly the most conservative of all colors.

GREEN communicates eagerness, growth, and a "let's go" attitude. In the United States, green is also closely tied to money. Consequently, green encourages interaction from the audience. Even a deep green or a blue-green (teal) will signify to the audience that their opinions are desired and that an invitation has been extended to them to express those ideas.

YELLOW, associated with a bright future, has an optimistic and active orientation. However, if left unchecked (overused), it can create anxiety. On flip charts, yellow is a color that is very difficult to see; it should probably only be used to highlight.

VIOLET or purple represents something magical or mystical. Violet brings with its charm the notion of something childlike or even unreal. Avoid using this color for critical business information. Don't be afraid to use it for humor, graphics, break information, and other similar non-critical details, however.

BROWN communicates solidity. However, we recommend that brown be used sparingly if at all: Most training is a call to action, and brown is definitely one of the most passive colors.

Two final observations are in order. Consider your presentational style when selecting the *shade* of color to use in the above instances. If you have a more animated style, select a darker shade to complement rather than further accentuate your style. On the other hand, if you have a more reserved style, don't be afraid to use the brighter colors to complement and augment your presentational style.

As a final warning, please keep in mind that too many colors will tend to give your flip chart a "circus" feeling — this will reduce credibility and overall effectiveness. Two colors per flip chart is generally a good rule of thumb, with one of those colors being the primary color and the other color used to highlight or headline the main text.

The Border

Borders can give your important messages the attention they deserve. Look at the example on the next page, and see how different the top and bottom illustrations are in their impact. Even individual words can be bordered, for greater emphasis.

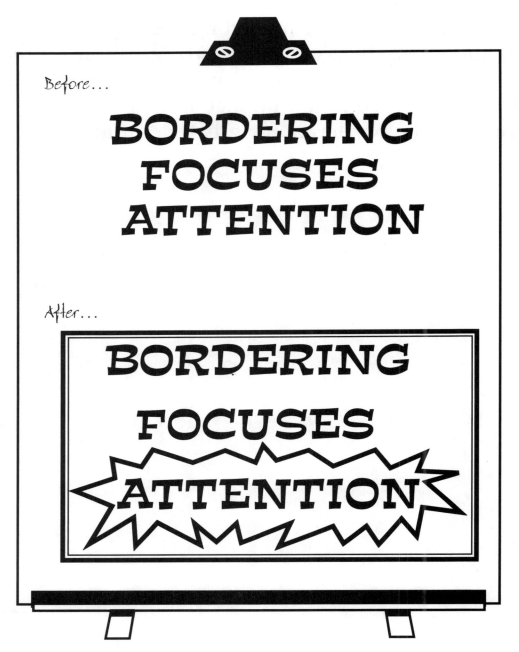

Want maximum impact? Use borders! Want maximum response? Use a variety of borders throughout your presentation. Here are some sample borders and practice pages. Go ahead — experiment!

29

Here's an example!

31

Now *you* try it!

Here's an example!

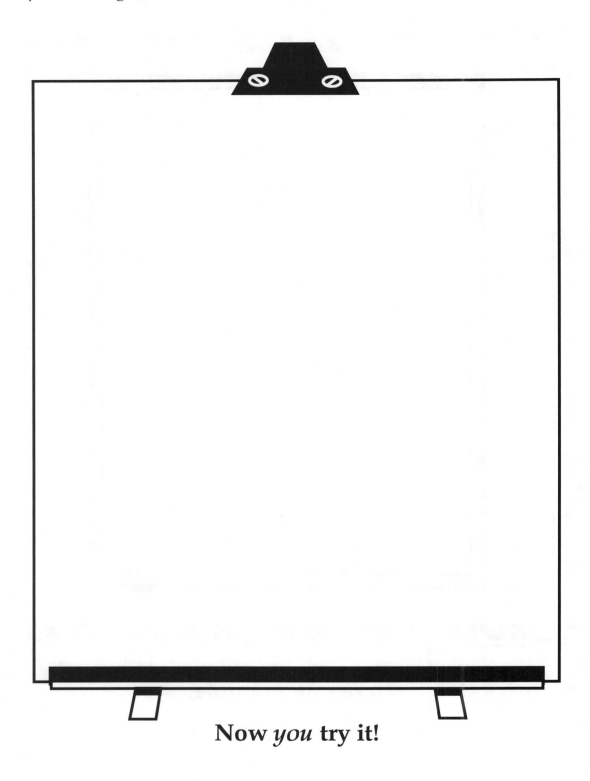

Now *you* try it!

Here's an example!

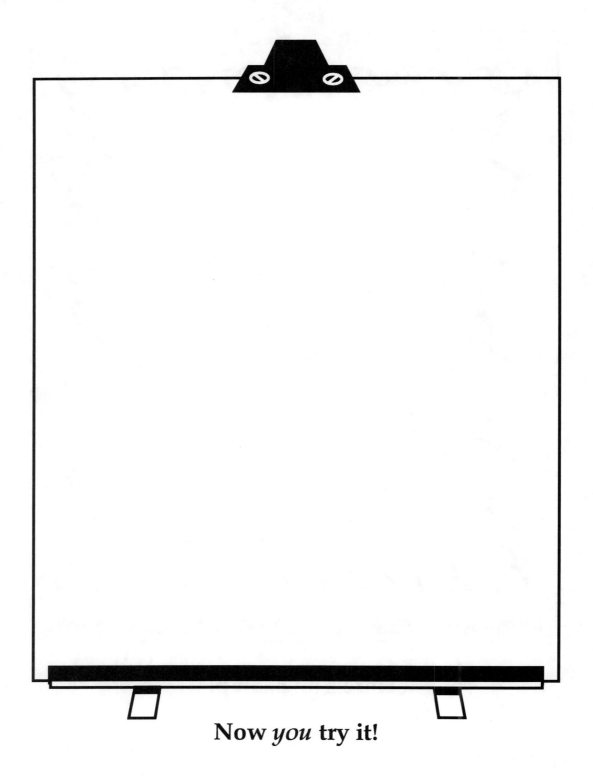

Now *you* try it!

Here's an example!

Now *you* try it!

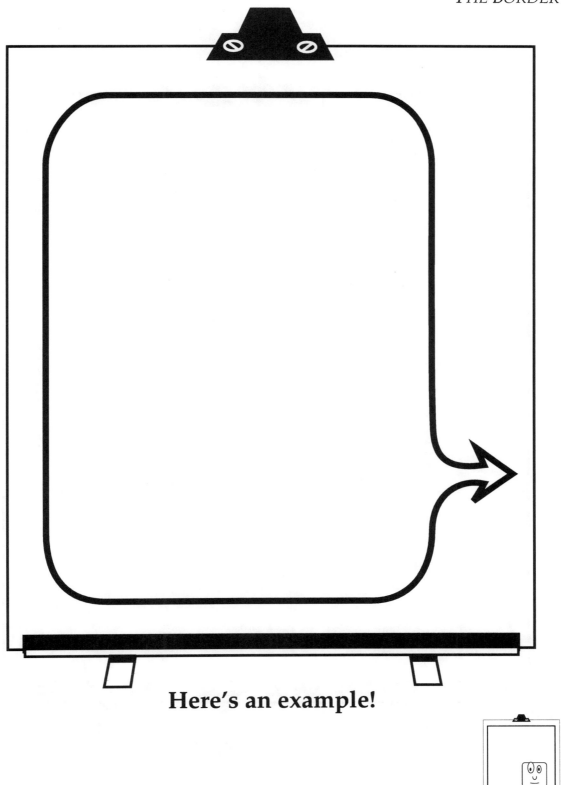

Here's an example!

39

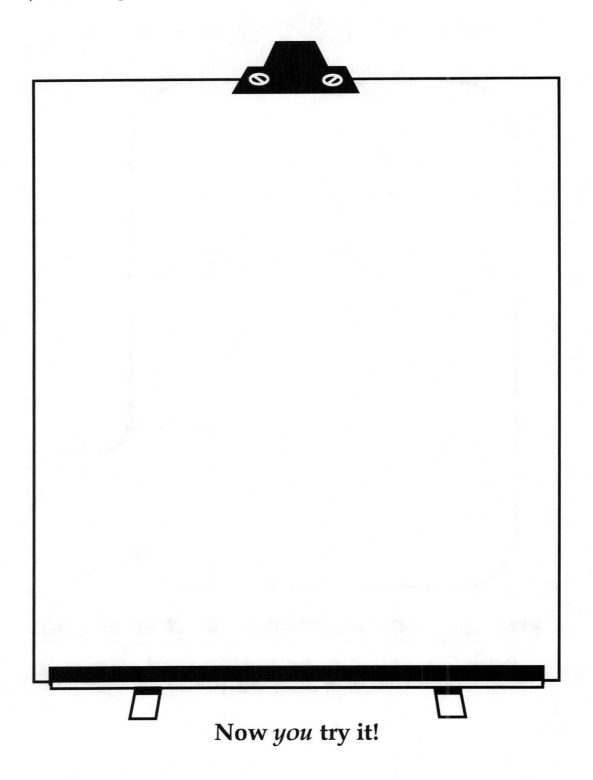

Now *you* try it!

Here's an example!

41

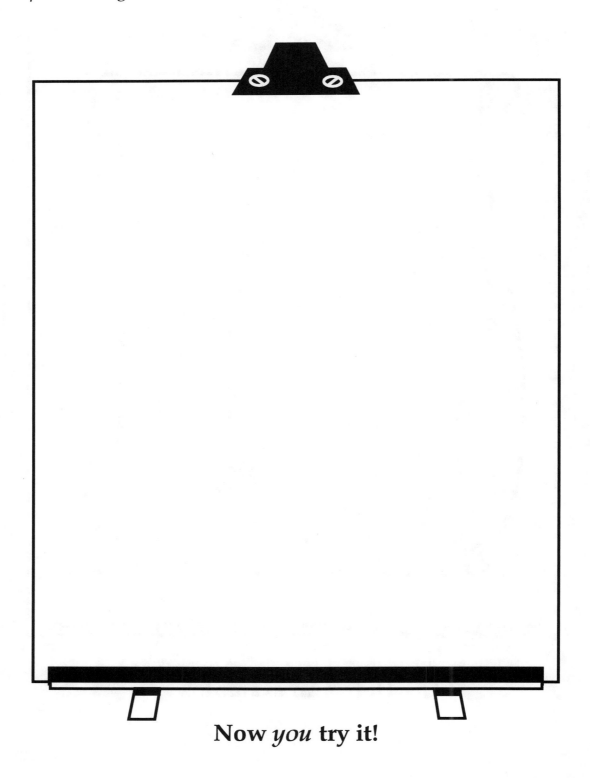

Now *you* try it!

Here's an example!

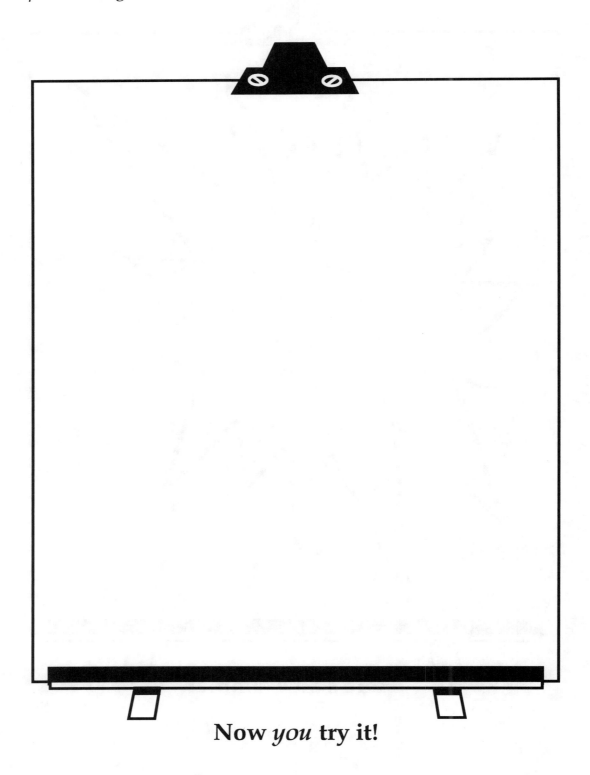

Now *you* try it!

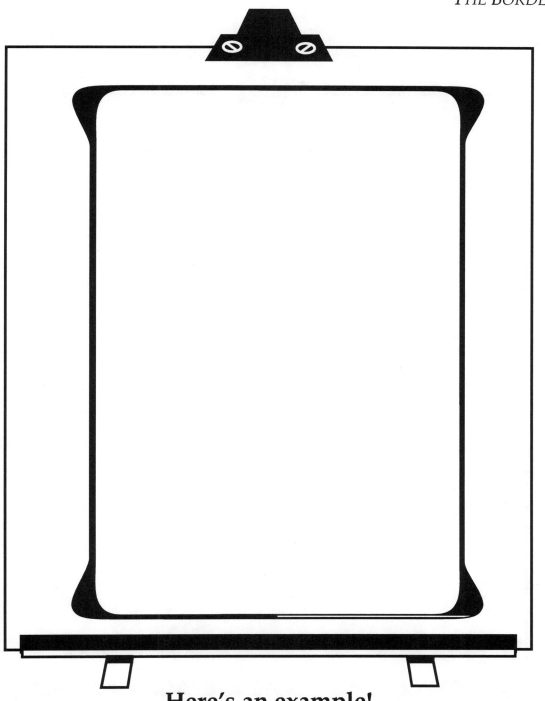

Here's an example!

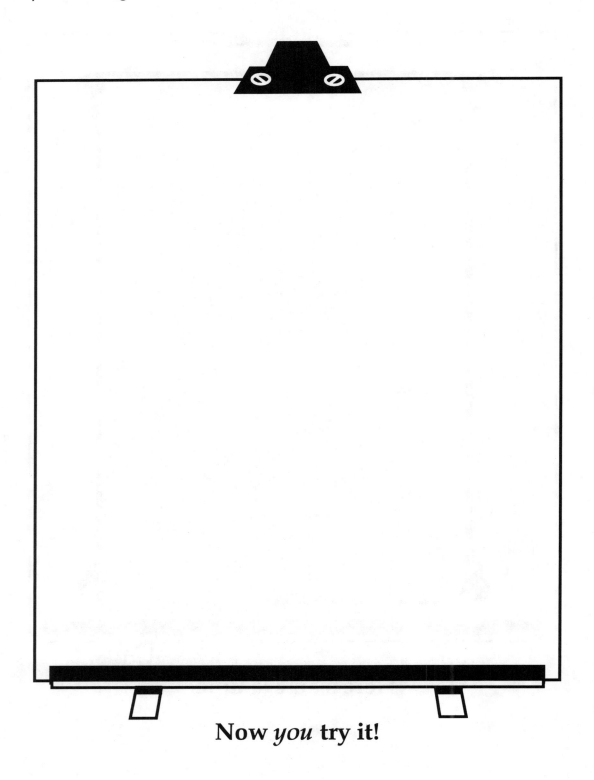

Now *you* try it!

THE LETTERING

AaBbCcDdEeFfGgHhIiJjKkLl
MmNnOoPpQqRrSsTtUuVv
WwXxYyZz1234567890

AaBbCcDdEeFfGgHhIiJjKkLl
MmNnOoPpQqRrSsTtUuVv
WwXxYyZz1234567890

AaBbCcDdEeFfGgHhIiJjKkLl
MmNnOoPpQqRrSsTtUuVv
WwXxYyZz1234567890

Interest can also be added to flip charts by varying the lettering styles you use, but we do not recommend using more than two lettering styles on any given flip chart. Try giving your flip chart heading a different lettering than the body of your flip chart; you will find everything more energetic. Make sure that your lettering is at least $1\frac{1}{2}$ inches high and that there are 2 inches between each line. Use as few words as possible to communicate your message. An easy way to get some consistency in your lettering is to always use lined flip chart paper. Avoid making your letters too tall because they will be

difficult to read. And use both upper and lower case letters for maximum variety and ease of readability.

You've probably noticed that you can write with either the narrow edge of the marker or the broad side of the marker. Notice in the following lettering samples how you can combine those two components to generate some creative combinations. Then move on to the next few pages, and practice with a marker in your hand.

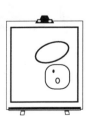

Observe how the text is on the upper ½ of the chart. The sight lines in most classrooms make it impossible to see the bottom 1/3 of the easel.

See how the inside border breaks into the outside border. Any time the outside border is broken by another border or graphic, the flip chart's energy increases!

Notice how the figure's eyes look back at the text. A viewer will always look at the figure first and then follow the figure's eyes to what the figure is looking at. By having the eyes looking at the text, the viewer's attention will be directed back to the text.

Appreciate how this inside border further focuses the attention of the viewer to the text message inside the border.

Take note of how the outer border focuses the attention of the viewer on that which is inside the border.

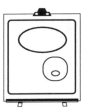

53

Now *you* try it!

Congratulations!

Go ahead and try one more!

Section Two:

Flip Chart Techniques

POSTING

We've provided what we hope is a very stimulating list of ideas for unique applications of the flip chart.

Do you want to be sure that your participants read your flip chart posting? Don't post it on the wall. Post it on the floor so that they have to walk over it or around it when they enter the room! Or if you must post it on the wall, hang it upside down!

And while thinking about those initial flip chart postings, try putting one up that simply says "Hi! I'm (your name)! And I'm Glad to Be Here!" You'll be amazed how communicating your attitude through a flip chart can really set the tone for the session.

And one also informing people where the restrooms are located really says to your participants that you care about them.

Want to hang flip charts on the walls easily without messing with masking tape? Try the new Post-it® Flip Chart pads currently available from 3M. They have a wide strip of glue across the backside top of every sheet!

Flip Chart Magic!

Refer to the Other Resources section in the back of this book for more ideas. Consider using Grip-A-Strip Wall mountings; by having these already on your training room walls, you can simply push up the flip chart pages under the metal strip, and they will be held in place. You can also pull gently on the flip chart pages to get them to come away easily from under the metal strip.

Do you have trouble getting your participants involved during your training? Post a flip chart page labeled "Volunteer Board," and then have people volunteer for various tasks (e.g., bringing people back from break, monitoring room temperature, etc.).

Do you struggle to keep people on task during training? Hang up a flip chart page labeled "Parking Lot." When someone brings up a question that you intend to deal with sometime later in the session, thank the participant for their question and write it on the flip chart page, "parking" it there until you can get back to it later in the session.

How about people who use the training room to complain about unrelated company issues? If you hang a flip chart page titled "Things We Can Do Nothing about in This Room," you'll have a place to write those voiced concerns.

Do the same thing with jargon. It's inevitable that people will use it, but this can be very frustrating to the newer employee. Create a "Jargon Board" so that you're ready whenever you or another participant lapses into the use of jargon. Write the word or phrase on the flip chart page and then explain its definition. You will have raised a potential problem to a very conscious level.

UNVEILING

Dave Arch's book entitled *Showmanship for Presenters* includes an entire chapter devoted to the fascinating process of *unveiling*. Here's a little excerpt from the beginning of that chapter.

> "The sculptor has completed a new piece of work, and it's about to be unveiled. A hush falls over the crowd as the covering is removed. People gasp as they see the piece of art for the first time. We love the removal of coverings. . . we love unveilings!"

What does an unveiling silently communicate? Doesn't it tell us we're about to see something valuable and out of the ordinary? You can use the unveiling technique to draw attention to an important training point. Write your message on a piece of chart paper and fold it in half by drawing up the bottom edge until it meets the middle and taping it. When you're ready to unveil that page, untape the lower half of the page and let it fall down — revealing your message.

If you are intrigued about the effectiveness of the unveiling technique, we suggest the following experiment: Take a full sheet of poster paper and letter a closing content message in large letters across its face (e.g., "Quality Is Important!" "We Can Do It!" etc.). Then fold the paper into fourths and place it in a large manila envelope. Hang the envelope from the ceiling at the front of your room, off to the side.

Someone is sure to ask what's in the envelope. Just tell them that you'll be opening it later. At the very end of your session, refer to the envelope by mentioning that you hung it there to remind you of a very important point you wanted to make. Remove the envelope from the string, open it, unfold the flip chart, and have the participants read the message aloud in unison.

You will feel the power of *unveiling* in a very dramatic way, but you will also have an excellent close for your session!

LAYERING

It's easy to reveal only part of the message at a time when using an overhead. You merely lay a piece of paper over the transparency and pull it down as you cover each aspect of your material. However, how could you use that same powerful delivery technique on the flip chart?

Try layering your content. Here's how it works.

Let's assume you have five points that you want to make. You would print your fifth point on the fifth sheet down from the top of your flip chart. You would then cut the fourth sheet a little shorter that the fifth sheet and print the second point you want to make at the bottom of that fourth sheet. You're probably beginning to see the pattern. The third sheet would then be cut shorter than the fourth sheet, the second sheet shorter than the third sheet, and the first sheet the shortest of all. Now you can turn all five sheets over the back of your flip chart and reveal only one sheet at a time beginning with the fifth sheet (and your first point). As each page is turned over the top of the flip chart, the next point is revealed until all five are listed on the easel (in order, reading from the bottom to the top).

Once you begin to understand the process of layering, you can use it in other ways as well. Recently, I asked participants to list drawbacks to the lecture-based approach to training. After filling the chart page with their responses, I reached over the top of the flip chart and pulled into view a secretly prepared header (only about 10″ long) that then served as a heading to the list the participants had compiled. The heading read, "Participant-Centered Training Seeks To Overcome…" This now became the heading of the new list. I made a powerful point about the role of participant-centered training by bringing this header into view, and helped change the perspectives of the participants from the initial assignment.

Keyholing is yet another variation on the layering process, first shared with me by Lynn Solem, a wonderful creative training techniques trainer.

In order to understand keyholing, let's set up an example. Before your participants arrive, make the following preparations: For a training session on the FIVE ways to increase your income, turn four blank pages over onto the back of your flip chart. On the fifth chart page on the pad, draw a box at the top middle of the page that says "WAYS TO INCREASE YOUR INCOME." (This can even be printed on a graphic of a dollar bill, with a border.)

Draw a border around the page, about three inches from each edge.

Now reach over the top of the flip chart and bring a blank page over on top of the prepared page. Using a pair of scissors, cut a hole in this sheet so that your heading box from the sheet underneath shows through. Then draw a different border around this page.

Reach over the top of the flip chart and bring the next blank page into view. Cut out a hole so that the first heading box you drew shows through. Then draw a border around this page, as well.

Continue this process until you have reached your final blank sheet. This now becomes the first sheet on the pad. However, due to the keyhole you've cut in this sheet, it looks as though the heading box is actually on this top sheet.

There will be oooooooh's and aaaaaaaaah's as you write down the first way to increase income on the top sheet and then flip it over the top of the flip chart.

Your participants will realize that the box is not on the top sheet at all. Continue turning the pages with each point you make, until you are on the last sheet in the series. You will find this to be an impactful way to use the flip chart.

As you experiment with keyholing, you will discover a few variations. One that usually surfaces rather quickly is the one where you make a frame on the very top sheet of paper and then cut the center out from the frame. You now have a frame that, because of its openness, allows you to draw your information on the second sheet. By reaching under the first sheet, you can tear off the second sheet for posting and you still have a framed area for continued writing on the second sheet, third sheet, and so forth.

Playing with some of these ideas will not only give you fresh energy as a trainer, but also will give your participants renewed enthusiasm as they see you using new techniques in your trainings. Variety is truly the spice of life (and training too)!

MULTIPLE SCRIBES

If you've ever tried to write on a flip chart while participants called out ideas, you know the problem. You just can't write as fast as they can talk! No one can.

And so, while you're writing, what are they doing? Many times they begin looking around the room or engaging in some other non-content-related activity. You lose the very energy you're trying to create with the flip chart.

It's much better to have one or more flip chart scribes step up to several flip charts (or several pieces of flip chart paper posted on the wall) and take turns recording participant ideas. However, be careful who you select to be scribes. Handwriting may be a problem, and there's nothing more uncomfortable than publicly embarrassing a participant by choosing someone and finding out early in the activity that he or she has a hard time spelling. The best way to avoid that painful situation is to make sure that the scribes are volunteers. If they are given a free choice about participating or not participating, such a situation will be easily avoided.

START-STOP-CONTINUE

By combining the flip chart with Post-it® notes so familiar to all of us, an excellent evaluation process emerges perfect for focus groups or other times in which an honest response is desired.

Distribute the Post-it note pads* so that everyone has an adequate supply. Have each person select a marker as well.

By way of illustration we will assume that a conference has just been completed and the conference committee is meeting to assess the effectiveness of the program. Begin by having each individual start writing on the Post-it notes in response to the following question: "Based on what we've just experienced with the conference, what do we want to be sure that we START doing next year?"

Each person writes only one idea per Post-it note.

While the participants write their responses, take a flip chart page and divide it into three columns, labeling the first column "START." If the group is large, post three flip chart pages on the wall and leave one entire page for START Post-it notes.

*Post-it® Keynote Pads prepared for this exact purpose are available through Creative Training Techniques International (800-383-9210).

If the group is not very large (no more than 20–25 people), begin by having one person share their START idea. After sharing the idea, the person stands and brings his or her Post-it note to the front of the room to put in the START column on the flip chart page. If anyone else had a similar idea, they are to all come at this time and stack (stick) theirs right over the top of the first one put in the column.

Then you ask for another START idea and repeat the process all over again with the new idea. When you are done with the START column (page), you will have a visual listing of all of the ideas as well as an excellent indication of how strongly the group felt about each one (by seeing how many people came up with the same idea).

If the group is large (more than 25 people), small groups can be used for the stacking process before moving into the process described above. This will allow even the most timid member of the group to get his or her ideas tallied in with the others.

After the completion of the START column, the process moves into the STOP column in which the same process is repeated in response to the question "In the light of our present conference experience, what should we *not* do at next year's conference?"

Finally, the process is repeated with the CONTINUE column by asking the question "From what we've just experienced in our conference, what should we be sure and *continue* to do at next year's conference?"

By the time this entire process has been completed, it will be a simple matter to record the information gathered and distribute the report to everyone. Everyone will be interested too because everyone will have had a chance to be heard!

Section Three:

Flip Chart Fun!

CHALK TALKS

"Chalk Talks" used to be quite the entertainment medium in the 1930s and 40s. The audience would sit and watch as the chalk talk artist drew a simple picture and then with a few lines changed that picture into something completely different. It was a mesmerizing entertainment medium because the picture would evolve in front of the audience until there was that sudden "aha!" moment in which the audience finally recognized what was being drawn.

Don't be afraid to take your time as you add your lines to complete your final picture. Some of the most captivating chalk talks had the picture completely drawn — the audience still didn't get the point until the picture was turned completely upside down! You'll find some of those on the next few pages, too.

Using the very first chalk talk as an example, you'd begin by putting the 2020 on the flip chart — printing it exactly as it appears on the drawing. Then you'd slowly add the lines until you had drawn the entire head of the person. The text is only there to help you frame your message as you do your drawing. It would not be on the completed flip chart.

Have fun as you explore the world of Chalk Talk! Along with the very simple chalk talks on various training subjects, you'll also find on the following pages a practice section so you can experiment.

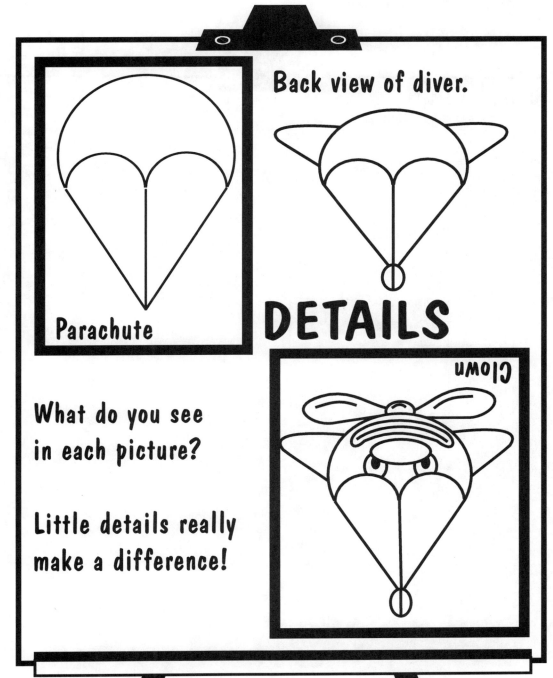

Parachute

Back view of diver.

DETAILS

Clown

What do you see
in each picture?

Little details really
make a difference!

Flip Chart Magic!

give it a try!

76

give it a try!

TRAIN THE TRAINER

WE MUST USE GRAPHICS!

Start with a "B"

Add a "U"

We think in pictures, not words. When I spell b-u-n-n-y, you don't see the word bunny . . .

Add an "N"

Add another "N"

. . . .but you see a bunny.

And add a "Y"

79

give it a try!

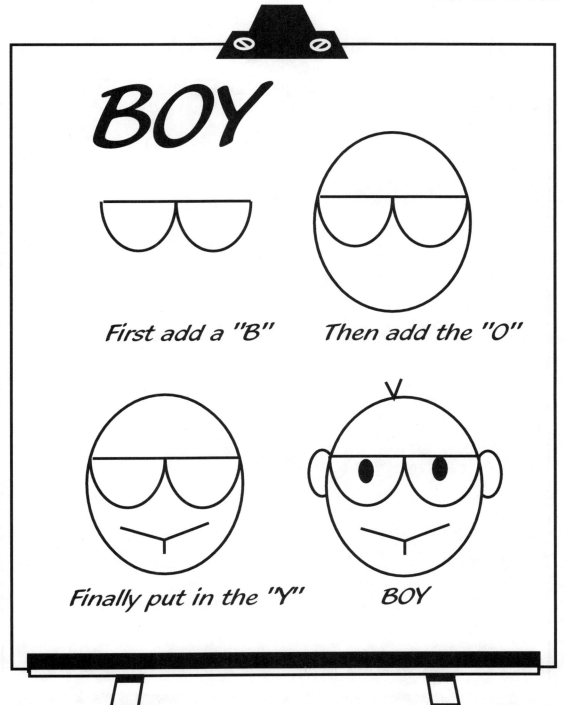

BOY

First add a "B"

Then add the "O"

Finally put in the "Y"

BOY

give it a try!

SALES

Upselling, from appealing to a person who wants to buy ice cream for a party . . . .

. . . . to selling them a CLOWN!

LET THEM TRY IT!

83

give it a try!

give it a try!

give it a try!

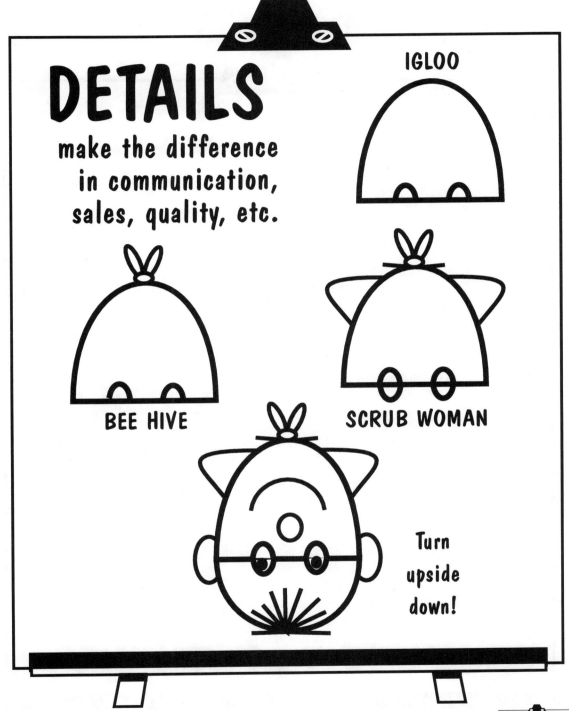

DETAILS

make the difference
in communication,
sales, quality, etc.

IGLOO

BEE HIVE

SCRUB WOMAN

Turn
upside
down!

give it a try!

DOODLES

Doodling was another popular form of entertainment in the 1940s and early 50s. The artist would draw what appeared to be an obscure design on the flip chart, and an audience would try to guess what had been drawn. It's a great activity for bringing a group back from break — getting those thinking juices flowing again. Better yet, draw the design before going to break, and promise to reveal its meaning following break. Give a prize to anyone who can figure it out. You'll find that the designs are so easy, your participants will want to try drawing them for family and co-workers!

You'll find fifteen easy doodle challenges on the next few pages. Draw the graphic (none of the text) on your flip chart, and have your participants try to guess what the figure represents. The text is only there so that you don't get stumped by any of the doodles!

3 little mice went out for a stroll, then 2 of the mice went down this

Looking upward through a grating, saw this guy standing, waiting.

YOU CAN DO

91

Ten feet of fine heavy rope — end view you see, I hope!

EVEN IF YOU CAN'T SEE THE FUN, THIS NEEDS CHECKING, DID YOU EVER SEE A COUPLE OF GIRAFFES NECKING?

A line it's true! Also a postcard — end view!

A SOLDIER AND A DOG HAVE JUST WALKED BEHIND A FENCE!

YOU CAN DO!

93

As a heavy
man sees
himself.

Section Four: Advanced Flip Chart Design

ADVANCED GRAPHICS

As your flip chart confidence increases, you will probably find yourself ready to move beyond the basic geometrical figures learned in the first part of this book and try some more advanced flip chart figures. When you're ready, the following pages will be waiting for you, complete with some great new graphic ideas, as well as practice pages so you can try your hand at the new figures.

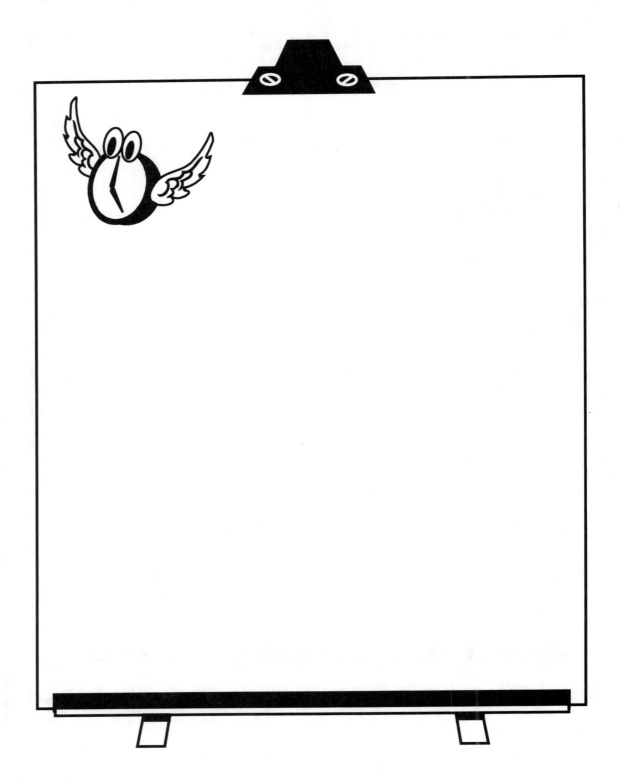

ADVANCED BORDERS

To add even greater variety to your flip charts, look at some of the NEW flip chart borders on the following pages. Then move ahead and try your own hand at drawing them!

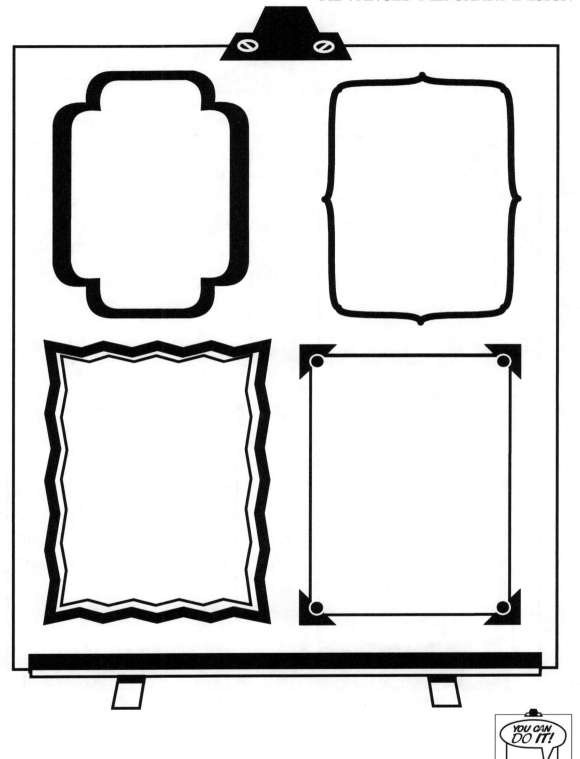

111

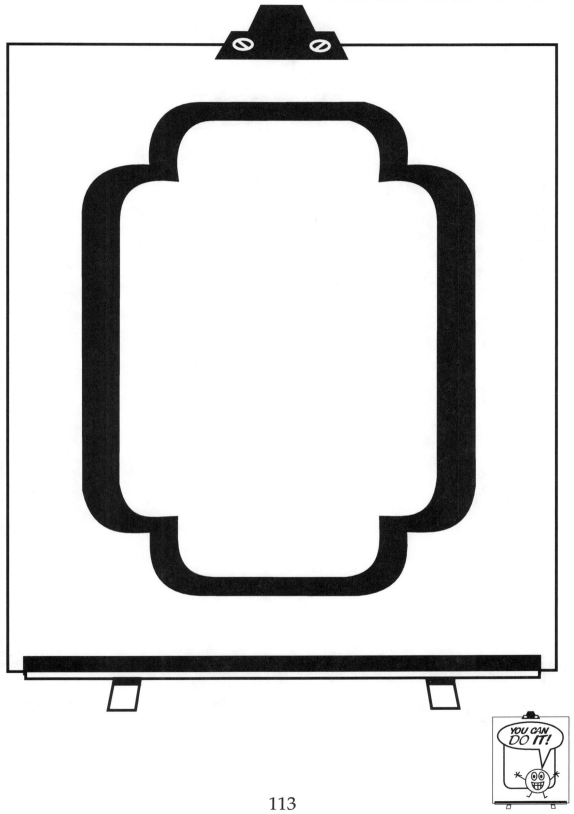

113

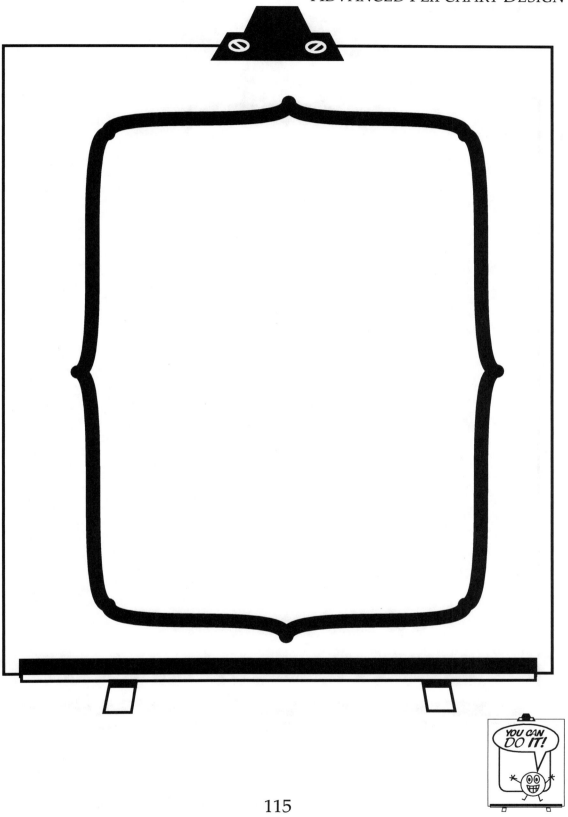

115

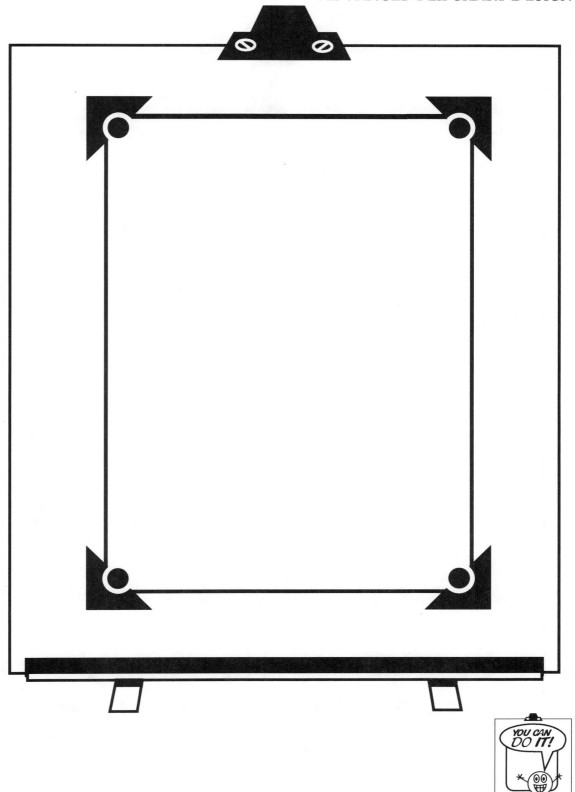

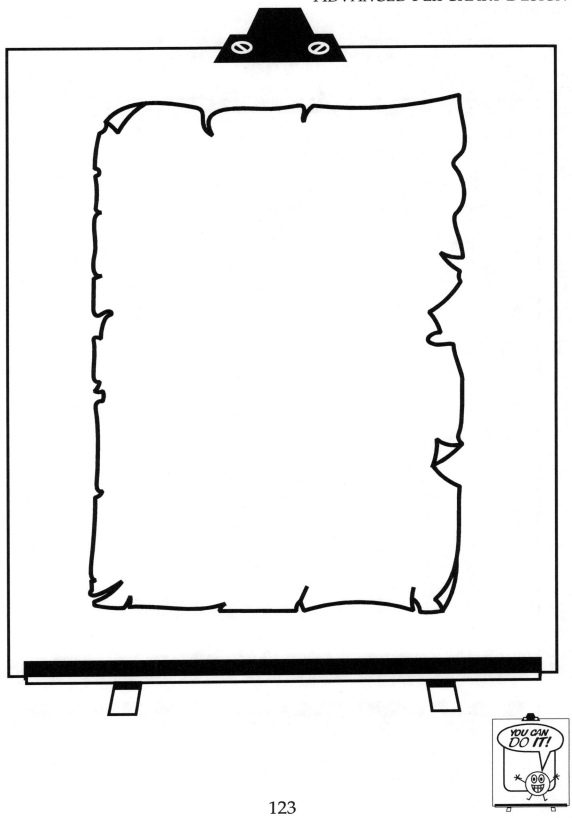

123

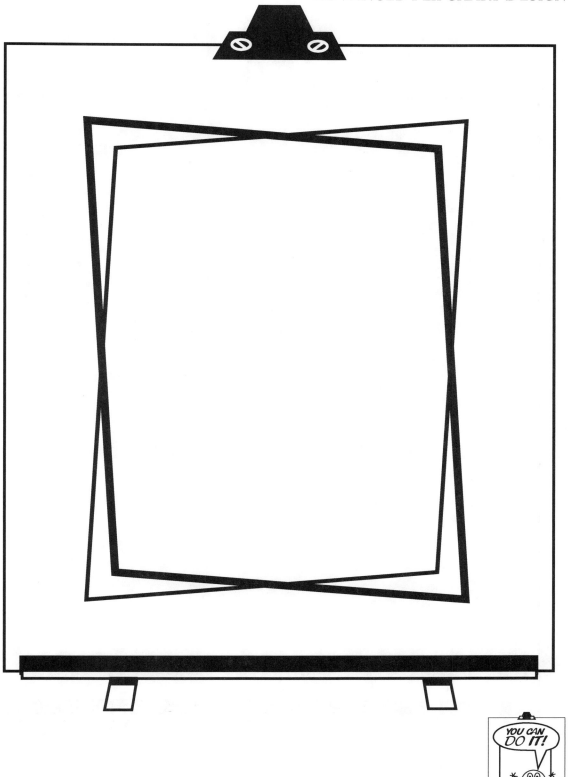

ADVANCED LETTERING

Other forms of lettering can also be used to bring greater variety to your flip charts. On this page and the next you'll find some NEW examples. Try your hand at them on the practice pages that follow.

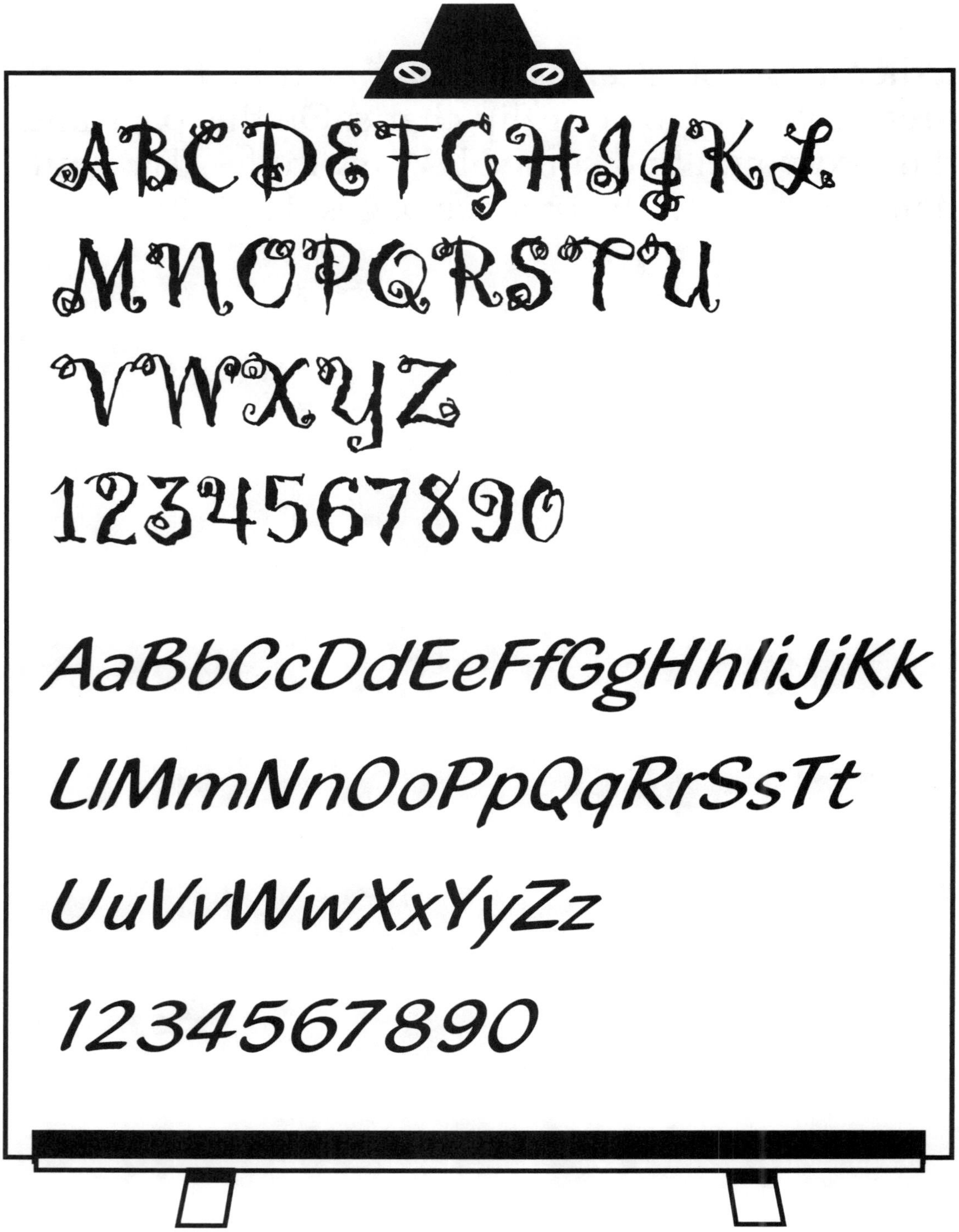

ABCDEFGHIJKL
MNOPQRSTU
VWXYZ
1234567890

AaBbCcDdEeFfGgHhIiJjKk
LlMmNnOoPpQqRrSsTt
UuVvWwXxYyZz
1234567890

AaBbCcDdEeFfGgHhIiJj
KkLlMmNnOoPpQqRr
SsTtUuVvWwXxYyZz
1234567890

AaBbCcDdEeFfGgHhIiJj
KkLlMmNnOoPpQqRr
SsTtUuVvWwXxYyZz
1234567890

AaBbCcDdEeFfGgHhIiJj
KkLlMmNnOoPpQqRr
SsTtUuVvWwXxYyZz
1234567890

Welcome

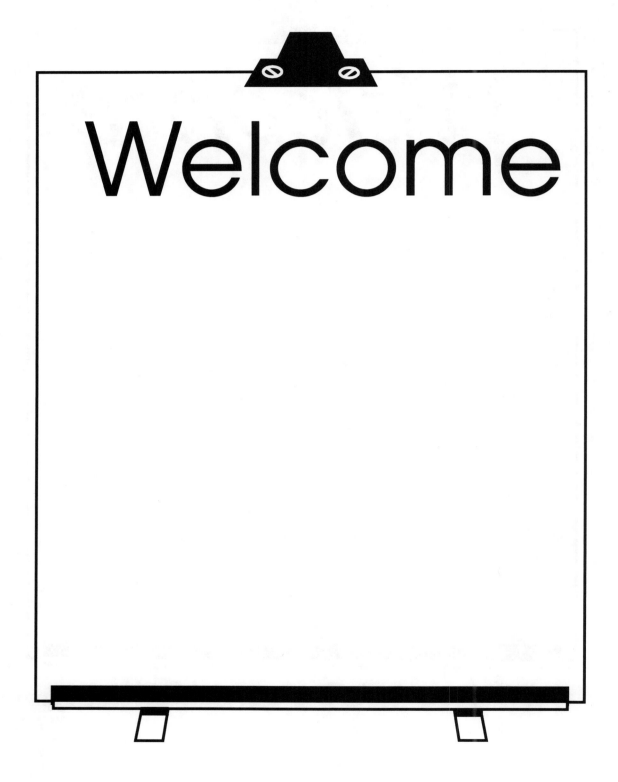

Welcome

WELCOME

Section Five

Bonus Section:

Flip Chart Transparency Masters!

FLIP CHART MASTERS

By combining your overhead projector with your flip chart, you really can have some fun and increase the interest and retention of your participants! Based upon your own content and the emphasis you want to make, select one of the seventeen transparency masters that follow.

Before your participants arrive, put the transparency on your overhead and project it onto your flip chart. Size it appropriately. Then lightly sketch the figure in pencil, using the projected image as your guide. If you sketch it lightly, your participants will not be able to see it from their seats, but *you* will be able to see it clearly if you are standing close to the easel.

Imagine your participants' reactions when you stride confidently to the flip chart and begin to slowly draw the picture. If you've ever watched one of those PBS shows where the artist paints the picture in front of the viewer, you know how captivating this can be. When finished, your picture will have direct link to your content and you will have a terrific opener or closer!

SALES

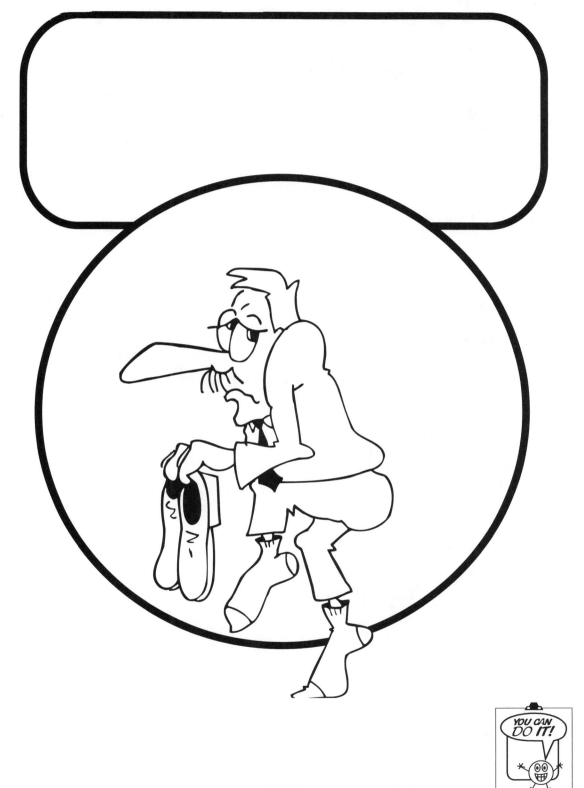

Section Six:

Other Resources

ADDITIONAL RESOURCES

- *Creative Training Techniques Handbook* by Bob Pike
  This book is THE textbook for training excellence! With over 200 pages of information about the participant-centered approach to training, this book is a must-have for every trainer's library. Available from

  Creative Training Techniques
  7620 West 78th Street
  Edina, MN 55439
  800-383-9210

- Creative Training Techniques Seminar
  This two-day seminar, open to the public, is held once a year at various locations throughout the United States. If you attend, you would get a chance to see how the trainer makes effective use of flip charts. You would also receive a very comprehensive course on how to transform *your* training into a more participant-centered learning experience. Contact Creative Training Techniques for a comprehensive brochure (800-383-9210).

- Creative Training Techniques World Wide Web site
  This ever-changing resource center can be found at http://www.creativetrainingtech.com When you visit the site, you will find a section entitled "Puzzlers for Presenters," which you can download. The monthly puzzles are perfect for putting on a flip chart for discussion while your participants get settled.

- Flip Chart Pointers
  You can break your participants' preoccupation by utilizing a wide variety of flip chart pointers. This particular one has a hand in a finger-pointing position, on the end of a large stick. Because the hand on the pointer is actually a crayon, it can be used to

write on the flip chart, too! It's available directly from the manufacturer at:

Tool Thyme
4108 Grace King Place
Metairie, LA 70002
504-887-5558

* *Flip Charts* by Richard C. Brandt
  Flip Chart Power by Bonnie Burn
  These two resources are available from:

Jossey-Bass/Pfeiffer
350 Sansome Street, 5th Floor
San Francisco, CA 94104
800-274-4434

* Games and Graphics Seminar
  This one- or two-day seminar is offered at the Creative Training Techniques Annual Conference, but is also available as a customized training program for your company. Call Creative Training Techniques for more information (800-383-9210).

* Grip-A-Strip Wall Mountings
  These aluminum strips are mounted permanently to the walls of your training room, so you never have to be bothered with masking tape again. Your flip charts can be easily inserted under the metal strip and just as easily removed. For more information, contact:

SACO
5016 River Point Road
Jacksonville, FL 32207
904-398-4290

* Keynote Pads
  These hexagonal Post-it note pads are available in two different designs. They are perfect for the Start-Stop-Continue exercise explained in this book. (Available from Creative Training Techniques: 800-383-9210.)

- Mr. Sketch Markers Flip Chart Set
These scented markers do not bleed through flip chart paper.
They come in only those colors that show up best on flip charts
(i.e., two black, two purple, two turquoise, one red, one blue, one
green, one brown, one magenta, and one dark green). Available
from Creative Training Techniques: 800-383-9210.

- Poster Printer
This machine takes an 8 1/2" X 11" drawing and enlarges it to flip
chart or poster size! For more information, contact:

  Varitronic Systems, Inc.
  600 South Highway 169
  Minneapolis, MN 55426
  612-542-1500

- Post-it® Flip Chart Pads
These pads with Post-it note glue applied on the back side of each
sheet are now available from most office-supply stores.

- *Presenter's EZ Graphics Kit* by Lori Backer and Michele Deck
This book will add additional flip chart ideas to your repertoire.
It's written by two excellent trainers and artists, and is available
from Tool Thyme (504-887-5558).

Flip Chart Magic!

- *Purpose Movement Color — A Strategy for Effective Presentations*
  This book by Tom Mucciolo and Rich Mucciolo concerns itself primarily with those ingredients necessary for electronic computer-generated presentations. It is available from the publisher at:

  MediaNet, Inc.
  305 Madison Avenue
  New York, NY 10165
  212-682-2250

- *Red Hot Handouts!* by Dave Arch
  Although this book focuses primarily on the creative design and use of handouts in presentations, many of the ideas can easily translate to the flip chart, too! Available from Creative Training Techniques: 800-383-9210.

- *Showmanship for Presenters* by Dave Arch
  Referenced in the "Unveiling" section of this book, this volume explores 49 techniques used by famous entertainers that have direct application to the training room. This book and all of Dave's training resources are available from Creative Training Techniques: 800-383-9210.

- Other resources by Dave Arch:
  Tricks for Trainers, Volumes I and II
  Tricks for Trainers Video Library (three volumes)
  The All-New Tricks for Trainers
  First Impressions/Lasting Impressions

  Dealing with Difficult Participants
  Creative Training Techniques for One-On-One Trainers
  Warming Up the Crowd
  Trainer Bingo
  Football Review

Your Own Ideas

YOUR OWN IDEAS . . .

The following pages are for you to use when you begin to assemble your favorite ideas. Collect them from several resources, including this book, so that you have the best ideas for flip chart work in one place. In the final analysis, these might become the most important pages in the entire book.

Your Own Ideas . . .

Flip Chart Magic!

Your Own Ideas . . .

Your Own Ideas . . .

Flip Chart Magic!

Your Own Ideas . . .

ABOUT THE AUTHORS

As a Senior Trainer for Bob Pike's Creative Training Techniques, **Dave Arch** has authored seven resource books for trainers and other presenters.

Drawing upon a ten-year background in personal and family counseling and twenty-five years' experience in the training industry, Dave presents his seminars and motivational keynotes before some 20,000 people each year in both corporate and conference settings.

Dave's clients include: The Nabisco Company, U.S. West Communications, United States Postal Service, Arizona Department of Health, Telecom USA, Washington State Hospital Association, National Food Service Association, Napa Auto Parts, Inc., Farmland Industries, and the Nebraska's Distance Learning Project.

Ivar Torgrimson brings to this endeavor twenty years of career experience in graphic arts. As you go through the book, you will quickly recognize his expertise in layout and design, as well as his wonderful talent as a freelance cartoonist (with over fifty published cartoons to his credit). As his friend for over thirty years, Dave Arch summarizes Ivar's contributions best when he says, "Ivar is certainly a master at his profession, but the quality I admire most is his ability to take what he knows and empower other non-artists like me to share in the fundamentals and consequently the joy of his craft." Ivar lives with his wife and two teenage children in Omaha, Nebraska.